# APHORIA

*poems*

## Jackie Clark

**Brooklyn Arts Press · New York**

APHORIA
© 2013 Jackie Clark

ISBN-13: 978-1-936767-17-5

Cover art by Shane McAdams. Design by Joe Pan.

Published in The United States of America by:
Brooklyn Arts Press
154 N 9th St #1
Brooklyn, NY 11249
WWW.BROOKLYNARTSPRESS.COM
INFO@BROOKLYNARTSPRESS.COM

Distributed to the trade by Small Press Distribution / SPD
www.spdbooks.org

Library of Congress Cataloging-in-Publication Data

Clark, Jackie.
  Aphoria / by Jackie Clark. -- First Edition.
    pages cm
  ISBN 978-1-936767-17-5 (pbk. : alk. paper)
  1. Poetry, American. I. Title.

PS3603.L36425A88 2013
811'.6--dc23

                                2012042109

10 9 8 7 6 5 4 3 2 1
FIRST EDITION

Acknowledgements:

Many thanks to the following journals where some of these poems appeared in earlier forms: *Leveler, Poor Claudia, Raleigh Quarterly, Realpoetik, Sink Review, Sixth Finch.*

The section *I Live Here Now* was published as a chapbook by Lame House Press in 2011.

# CONTENTS

Things moralize, to meet

my expectation, because I want advice
on how to live.


—Catherine Wagner

(

)

We Gather At Night

( )

Under the

ammunition

of the red room

I am unwrinkling

gallantry with a

blindfold

You are

forcing the hatch

and bounding

the floor in rubber

The idea of us

is my palm

held up parallel

to my face

( )

The coyote-
lemon horizon

returns

I limit

the tea-trade

and disperse

expectations

throwing them

by the handful

at everything

I remember

but I don't

remember much

( )


We enjoy

the prospect

of gathering

lightning bugs

The foibles of men

poke around under

rocks, applying

meaning

to their solitary

spacewalk

while fingers

hypnotically roll

invisible balls

back and forth

between

their tips

( )

All doors do

something different

and some

mornings

I think of you

and think of my

collections

of spotted-land

rolled flat

onto the walls

in rooms

where I've once

lived

( )

I am asking
that you not
find anything
wrong, that
your skin be
palpable and wide
that you unfold
the futon and not
make eye contact
Your imposed
instruction
doesn't say wait
but nothing
is ever said
so I know
what you are
not saying
I want to gather
your skin, so
loose and unassertive

This basement

has windows

I open

when you are

not looking

( )

Eagerness

arranges olives

and aged Gouda

Ties wired-

chiffon in bows

around all

the dark-haired

girls   Our mouths

hollow

with expectation

It is not your turn

to be the bashful one

You should point

out the snails, you

should say

look up, look up

All occurrences

are muted

and starred until

you remember

there is an outside

out there

( )


White flesh
is the first thing
that flashes
Our first
morning after
many mornings
I touch you
because you
are a person
and I am a person
Through the wall
keys make noise
and autonomous
appendages
make lists
The amount
of times
my fingers
have ran through
different hair
It feels so good
to be breathed
upon

( )

Regrowth

has captured

the upward

mobility you've

so carefully

tended

Your hammer

ensures

my silhouette

Right now

the sun is

stronger than

it is not

The cement-

footed lamppost

obliges me

with its company

( )

X marks the spot
is a cautionary tale
as with the arrow
that imposes
precision  The sun
goes in
and there is relief
The sun comes out
and there is relief
What else is the sky
but blue
and yet I love
the weather
today, you say
Totally anticipatory
you say
There was something
so tender about
imagining you
listening
to the radio in the dark

like that, you say

I fell asleep right in

the middle of my book

in slow detail

( )


The door

remains open

and asks you

not to resist

the key

The grass

at night

is moist

under our feet

Everything

is well-

intended and

impossible

I will leave

here

with a name

I could not

have given

myself

( )


We have spent

the day

collecting

like mercury

Our shiny

beaded pool

Our independent

gauge

I am only

every adjective

I can't

think of

and still

you are well-fitted

from bone to skin

It is menacing

to acquire fences

to drive down

from the mountain

day after day

(

)

The City Salutes Itself

( )


A face covered with bees exists in an open field.
                        The caged-queen atop
the skull,

an experiment in the likelihood of behavior, the predictable swarm
misrepresented by the lone bee,

                        a dot captured on hand
like an unnamed land mass lost north of the arctic. The video

swells. My unadorned social arm

prickles in the dark.

( )


We refer metaphorically to the house being on fire, to the obvious

        connection between the fire and leaving the house. The metaphor is
easily applicable.

Stocks fall
victim to this thinking, as do those with a strong sense of moral repair.

( )

We move
quickly through imaginary tangents,

speculate on the *how* as opposed to the *what*. Let's talk about
the thing instead of the other thing

or coil yellow rope on warehouse floors as testaments
to themselves.

We assume understanding and are obliged to roll our eyes, reintroducing
calamity to that which instigates.

( )

There is an inside
here,

a doomed curvature where blackened starlings construct lunar lines.
There are final moments

in the snow where
        a greenhouse garden grows fooled into production.

This is the measure of success, that which moves yonder without hesitation,
that which is misunderstood when not deductive.

                    The internal sense of tending deconstructs the ritual. Those final
moments in the snow

are not submission,
        they are the pleasure of creating condensation where none should be.

( )


Here
          men and women

     string
rings, sliding their smooth surfaces from end to end.

Tonight our faces are involved in intense conversation.

     We speak
of things we can hold, things we have held, and what we hope to trash.
One could draw a house around our faces without needing to lift the pen.

Cream wool parts and makes pathways,
          knitted or shagged,
                    wound-tight or pushed low, not as

much a divide
as oxygen coursing lower.

                    As in, survival supplies for all. As in,
                              following expected drama.

( )

The city is naked.

It spends time on open, on record. The city churns
        arranging seeds.

The speaker system
        underground encourages vigilance.

There are show tunes to the rhythm of quarters shaking in plastic. The city
sometimes dresses in white and asks for money.

The city is sometimes the city
        somewhere else and people fly to it with money from machines
in their pockets and mental lists of things within their power to conquer.

        The city

                        says
I've read that, I know that, I have that.

When the city returns
from the city somewhere else it relays this triumph. It makes electronic
representation.

                The city salutes itself.

( )


The mounted versus its absent prefix,
    adding brevity to interaction.

Each face made of clay. Each greeting the greeting of the first time. I only

know what I receive, and only then know it once.

Walking up a stairway is like this.

So sure of the reaction between nerves and brain, between brain
    and cataloged history.

            Categorically, Sundays are made for this.

Each section needs a subject.

                    Each subject, flotation.

( )


You take cover.

     You tent the roof.

I'll walk the rows while wooden bodies pose over mechanical inclines, limber

over paper and press and shy

     turns.

( )


Gather the pocket, the slouched arc.

      Our
            arms make rounds,

make shapes to pull
forward, that ask what remains outside to come in, that ask

warm to touch warm.

Most grateful, most private plea, be spared
            the embarrassment of expectation.

( )


Upon introduction
        of the knife, the knife

must be used
        shortly after.

Quiet

will again be fortified.

The turning axis reaches the window in bird song.

                I am reporting anything
        I can remember.

( )

The wind-turned canvas sign of the store, the rusty metal
    left exposed.
The place from which we exit. Anecdotes prosper.

We are capable of socializing
    in public.
Our mouths
alternate.

The mythology is that is it perpetually morning
    though we cannot see the sun in the east.

The mythology leads us forth through rain washed streets, exercises
    under-trained aesthetics,
the histories of other mythologies

    crafted in oil and charcoal

the accumulation of individual minutes against the
    obsessively staccato sensibility of the smallness

    of an object moving through space and time.

Time is not quantified in-between.
    The soft, brown canvas wraps around.

( )


The rocket carries human
persons.
Is propelled over blue. The land

is a means to water,
            a splash as graceful as iconic. The bodies

wait for recognition
to set in.

( )


Beds become filled, beds become emptied. We ask for no judgment
    unless it is favorable.

The insurmountable illusion of interchangeability:
    canary,           constitution,           combustion.
Stockpiles of generative combinations

and laudatory specifics.

We see this.

The clamoring wind's ideas of unending cold. Ordinary folks doing
ordinary things inside their homes.

When I sleep, the cats sleep.

Each day remains possible because a sense of the rest is lost.
    What happens next is what happens.

( )


The water believes that the wood standing along it stands for it alone,
    breaching the homeway.

Wheels spoke over the wood

but take turns too fast and meet
ground. Rocks exist just for the water.

The sun looks loving and available
        but there are conditions set before the sun, before it

can shadow among objects.

( )

The fever flushes the body.

It asks to keep the streets empty. It asks to be fed the order
with which communication is most successful.

The greeting.          The question.          The brief narrative.
Or rather the silence.

The instructive interaction of body frame.

Collecting plastic, you introduce ephemeral value.

You don't
even dust them off

and unapologetically do not stop their
construction.

( )


The briefest of art teeming
        through mechanical doors. Everything

                                    is not proportional.

The motion to represent this feeling would be rounded arms.

It would be repetitive and gentle like touching someone's back
        for the first time.

I want to greet the striking resemblance of apes, things likened to
        floodgates and abrupt departures.

( )


Boldness is always an option
        against reproduced arsenals for the tolerant and amused. The women
in their youth.

Something really awful could happen at any moment.

The weather is a symptom of duress.

Ultimately I want to oblige the family tree. At least suggest
that care
                has not been in vain.

This metaphor is something akin to releasing a parachute only it

presupposes
        a parachute exists.


                The land's grid looks simple and devastating
in its browns and greens from up here.

( )


Decorative artillery is the subject
of many conversations, though artillery is always referred to
as defense,

a gesturing simpatico

with underground tunnels. No one disputes the necessity
of a sword at arms length.

( )


The field is wide.
     The field is empty.

Injustice is debatable,
                as is worth,
    or the rounded blowfish.

My excuse is your excuse.

How does one anticipate automation
    when there is so much to be
suspicious of.

( )


The falling white,
each pore
     open to dynasty and decline.

Even the cavern of wonder is without wonder.

If I had wanted to be you
          I would.

(

)

I Live Here Now

( )


Of that which is completely empty,
which resists objection,
what sonic combustion,
what din of fork on plate,
of sky up above,
which corner amends previous corners,
which ear turned outward,
a leaning in that ends in ink, lends against sinking,
a promise to promise nothing more than a warm tub,
an elongated back,
whispering is much easier in the dark,
what relation describes the proximity,
describes penmanship in the shape of tree,
for want,
for expulsion of emotion, wrought iron,
unabashedly arguing the objective,
the never naming,
the already having named,
we spend wallets of time for talking,
on time to anticipate together,
there is no color for that,
the community makes all colors,
makes reaction unable to be gauged,
who institutes anything,
what dried pepper,
what pie of your eye,

yet the morning happens every morning,
someone somewhere wakes up,
looks through the curtains at the sky,
what body is the body,
now it sleeps
and holds in its thoughts,
what is time in this equation,
how it leans,
how time is smarter now than it was then,
not unabstract,
not unlike a calling,
a construction that builds itself into itself,
how the happy heart is scooped out like an avocado pit,
simply removed and appropriated,
how the opposite of everything,
even without the pay off,
which is the pay off,
is central

( )

Gliding steel,
absolute power crowd,
strong legs maintaining distance,
it is always this morning,
the patterned hole has a surprise ending every time,
I invite the camel and the wheel,
those strong legs keep their balance in transit,
they make the case for further transit,
for art museums in the mountains,
for casual lines,
for poems in small pieces,
what outside stimuli speaks to the ear machine,
the internal accordion emitting only hums of air,
when the dry is drying,
when the flex is flexing,
the cold street isn't as cold

( )

Intuition swallows the violin,
open and close,
invitation asks for response,
the small marginalia,
I feel bucketed by the noise,
it gateways,
it opens this bridge,
I flow upstream,
I float between this space and that,
who chips away the ice,
makes narrative in the abstract,
what I want to tell you that I couldn't just as easily tell myself,
this hook that transmits radio frequencies,
so much for a call to arms,
bearing love for whatever is the object of current love,
placed gently in anticipation of completion,
a home with spoons,
a home involved with the idea of being home,
a place toward which all energy flows,
we gather its encompassing patience,
lend shoulders to other shoulders,
distrust the night,
making what we have always thought we should make,
a collective sense of success for living inside our bodies,
inside the jurisdiction that speaks to our collective inadequacies,
for want of elocution and receipt,
my voice through someone else's ears

( )

Overflow,
the repository gathers,
thick water,
a falling in public,
of private space engaged with surface areas,
even with labels, each retelling discloses pent up attributes,
it is vague,
it is a story of my person, my compass,
guided by a piece of string,
situational relations,
neck bone open to the sky,
touching is so abstract,
the sky space unto the new window,
meteorological cures,
private nights,
departure embrace before fleeing,
before adjudicating gardens,
miles of scenic travel erasing the decade,
why betray the inner ocean,
why invite commentary,
or the inventory of unused powers,
whether to lay low or prowl,
to let laurels rest where they deserve to rest,
formulas institute formulas,
love institutes love,
for all the wandering ,
a stationary place pours,
out from within

( )

What gut feeling strings out the lights,
tests every bulb,
no matter what, always the train that carries me away,
the door chimes impressed on the walls,
my wall a projectionist's preference,
communication reflexive and perfunctory,
car wheels, there is perpetually nothing,
the physical depth of holes in the ground,
what geometrical figures outline my conversations,
cultural retaliation,
collecting social realities and reorienting in accordance,
I don't know how to slow down the molting,
how to steady my left hand on the notebook,
a will with very little forethought,
if I say I want to touch face am I saying something more,
even my vocabulary doesn't know,
if I say I want to touch eyes what am I asking you to see

( )


What moves across the country snow roads,
closing behind the otherness that is out there,
the frantic notes,
undisturbed promises,
geographical cures,
one soured foot in front of the other,
how brave to leave it all behind,
to expect nothing will ever be better until you leave,
how swift we move when collectively so light,
how soundless vocabulary whips though our chemistry,
what black and mysterious night there is out there,
all day,
what doesn't know of the hidden anymore,
belief in the project of never,
never knowing of who approves,
why you are lonelier than the tip of any mountain top

( )

Continued,
the space,
exhausted return,
we sweater up,
color falls,
eye contact makes me blush,
a photo is only good if you remember to take it,
the act alone constructs the memory net,
the actual picture,
antiques of modern life on bedroom walls,
sex as orientation,
we want to believe that what we are in relation to is unique

( )


Liberty ports adjusting to siphoned rivers,
counting the moments like counting the moments,
everybody has them,
light-headed Monday,
at least goodbye is complete,
at least the personal has been extracted,
has no reason to ever return,
my head interrupts,
sends vertigo behind my eyes,
what is there to revere about porcelain,
I'm not sure what awaits,
perhaps this is an admonishment of the foundry,
exchanging windows for windows,
a higher ceiling,
varying degrees of vault,
I rally to daydream,
it is not a crime to stay until the end,
only a preference,
my brief terminology,
rounding the docks,
the sound of metal bobbing in water,
I will arrive when I arrive,
who knows what it will be like,
how fast the day will pass,
who I will sing face to

( )

When the things at hand aren't properly identified,
we use deterrents,
make distractions,
ignoring the framework at large,
we make new friends,
avoid journalism,
expound private upon private,
inch legs and arms closer to other legs and arms,
the windowed room without direct sun light,
highlighting its high ceilings,
receptionless space,
what throat clearing goal are we working toward,
images of faces behind books,
fabled romance not actual,
when does the primitive factor in,
I do not know how to describe the philosophy of affect,
taking every square peg and introducing it to circle,
the first-person magical,
I cannot hear the spheres sing,
the world not populated with ghosts,
but people who romanticize their transit,
haunting and recontextualizing,
never having been to the highest point of anything

( )


What asks to be rotated,
radial circumference,
I couldn't imagine the boxes being packed,
couldn't look in the closet once I knew they were there,
the back entrance as your exit,
wires dislocated from speakers,
all this while someone may or may not be looking,
over my shoulder,
the air patterns here so nauseatingly neutral,
everyone thinking thoughts to themselves,
the moment of internalization,
the concept of conception,
what to do when you feel,
your heart is exploding into the mattress,
listening to the drone of the busted speaker,
where is the whole-hearted heart,
its province of immutables

( )

Swallow locations,
minefields detonate as per order,
prolong the anti-effacing,
prolong the darkness,
how quickly we forget,
the new glass I sit behind,
you who lacks my physical sense,
how many late nights,
when did this become a quantified investment,
but I am lucky,
no longer interested in guiding your horse,
I might as well be alone in a field,
I might as well let my tits hang out,
the rest of this is just some fabricated protocol,
and I know how to fuck myself

( )

Reading finger tips,
the strength in which they press,
that which springs forth without intention,
out of context what does the warning bell signify,
my person in relation to others,
who can be faulted for that,
there are enough instances when the wire just isn't long enough,
to reach the wall,
why struggle,
I barely have time to think about what it means to be alive,
it's not unrequited,
it's only sitting alone watching all these other feeling-faces,
wondering who would answer should I choose to knock,
how inefficient,
we should only be able to know what we are,
thinking from one moment to the next,
that familiar feeling-face sits inside its own difficulty,
curling wire,
making decorative love,
adorning without pleasure,
valuing the clear-spoken,
cradling the objects

( )

I can picture the desert but not your place in it,
conditioning of season,
how to read social cues,
I recall your Polaroid,
what perfect placement, lacking candidness,
you described and I listened,
the utmost indication of intimacy,
why fire these moments,
everything is always slightly better elsewhere,
where I grind my teeth in impatience,
I am not above the gathering,
the place where acquaintances convene,
forging in capacities of subsequent love,
everything subsequent,
such knowing is just cause for suddenness,
division from sun,
sun which I have been privy,
sun which touches distant yous at the same time,
the routine of posture,
routine of sweat,
this urgency escapes me,
I try to tell it how pleased I am to be right here,
to have seen the Polaroid,
one part memory house,
one part sweater

( )

If I dream of a boat,
what to make of the water,
an abbreviated holiday,
I dream of fields but even then know I am inventing symbols,
how much like an arrow,
revisitation is an emotional crime,
I dream of working,
I can ruin any affection,
classic wherewithal,
not loose upon the crowd,
not looking for a familiar face,
avenue after avenue does not ask me to know them,
neither do you,
I look deep into people's eyes when they are looking,
the other way,
a glimmer of invitation,
should we always assume that we are welcome,
for as long as we want to be welcomed?

( )


We travel with wine,
supersede the ocean floor,
alone,
knowingly,
and unknowingly,
as is how such things get decided,
endless gaze,
that deep dream hole and local color,
we can all just talk on the phone anytime we want,
so many years without domestic sanctuary,
what is a safehouse if not a house of one,
playful gone-gone,
no longer missing actual intimacies but imagined ones,
the serpent narrative,
repent,
repent,
all your gathered wears,
all the careful fashioning,
elegy,
elegy,
all those stories go up into the air and die

## ABOUT THE POET

Jackie Clark is the series editor of Poets off Poetry and Song of the Week for *Coldfront Magazine*. She is the recipient of a 2012 New Jersey State Council on the Arts Fellowship in Poetry and is the author of three chapbooks: *Office Work* (Greying Ghost Press), *Red Fortress* (H_NGM_N), and *I Live Here Now* (Lame House Press). Jackie lives in Jersey City and can be found online at nohelpforthat.com.